I0454888

# CRIMINAL JUSTICE

## EXCERPTED

FROM THE

2011 ANNUAL REPORT

OF THE

## CONGRESSIONAL-EXECUTIVE

## COMMISSION ON CHINA

ONE HUNDRED TWELFTH CONGRESS

FIRST SESSION

OCTOBER 10, 2011

Printed for the use of the Congressional-Executive Commission on China

Available via the World Wide Web: http://www.cecc.gov

U.S. GOVERNMENT PRINTING OFFICE

71–190 PDF                    WASHINGTON : 2011

For sale by the Superintendent of Documents, U.S. Government Printing Office
Internet: bookstore.gpo.gov   Phone: toll free (866) 512–1800; DC area (202) 512–1800
Fax: (202) 512–2104   Mail: Stop IDCC, Washington, DC 20402–0001

# CRIMINAL JUSTICE

## *Findings*

- During the Commission's 2011 reporting year, the Chinese government waged a broad-scale crackdown on human rights advocates, lawyers, bloggers, writers, and democracy activists. In early 2011, Chinese public security officials detained more than 200 advocates in a campaign that appeared related to official sensitivity over recent protests in the Middle East and North Africa and to an anonymous online call for so-called "Jasmine" protests within China.
- Harassment and intimidation of human rights advocates and their families by Chinese government officials continued during this reporting year. Public security authorities and unofficial personnel illegally monitored and subjected to periodic illegal home confinement human rights defenders, petitioners, religious adherents, human rights lawyers, and their family members. Such mistreatment and abuse were evident particularly in the leadup to sensitive dates and events, such as the Nobel Peace Prize award ceremony in December 2010 and the "Jasmine" protests of early 2011.
- Chinese officials continued to use various forms of extralegal detention against Chinese citizens, including human rights advocates, petitioners, and peaceful protesters. Those arbitrarily detained were often held in psychiatric hospitals or extralegal detention facilities and subjected to treatment inconsistent with international standards and protections found in China's Constitution and the PRC Criminal Procedure Law.
- Chinese criminal defense lawyers continue to confront obstacles to practicing law without judicial interference or fear of prosecution. In cases that officials deemed "politically sensitive," criminal defense attorneys routinely faced harassment and abuse. Some suspects and defendants in sensitive cases were not able to have counsel of their own choosing and some were compelled to accept government-appointed defense counsel. Abuses of Article 306 of the PRC Criminal Law, which prescribes criminal liability to lawyers who force or induce a witness to change his or her testimony or falsify evidence, continue to hinder effective criminal defense.
- In February 2011, the National People's Congress Standing Committee reviewed and passed the eighth amendment to the PRC Criminal Law, which reduced the number of crimes punishable by the death penalty to 55 crimes. The reduction signaled the first time the Chinese government has reduced the number of crimes punishable by capital punishment since the PRC Criminal Law was enacted in 1979. International organizations and the state-run media pointed out that courts rarely,

if ever, applied the death penalty for the 13 crimes no longer eligible for capital punishment.

*Recommendations*

Members of the U.S. Congress and Administration officials are encouraged to:

○ Press the Chinese government to release immediately advocates who are in prison or detention and to adhere to fair trial standards and ensure procedural protections for the approximately 40 human rights advocates in cases that have already gone to trial.

○ Support the establishment of exchanges between Chinese provincial law enforcement agencies and U.S. state law enforcement agencies to study policing, evidence collection, inmate rights, and other criminal justice reforms currently underway in China.

○ Press the Chinese government to adopt the recommendation of the United Nations (UN) Committee against Torture to investigate and disclose the existence of "black jails" and other secret detention facilities as a first step toward abolishing such forms of extralegal detention. Ask the Chinese government to extend an invitation to the UN Working Group on Arbitrary Detention to visit China.

○ Call on the Chinese government to commit publicly to a specific timetable for its ratification of the International Covenant on Civil and Political Rights, which the Chinese government signed in 1998 but has not yet ratified. Press the Chinese government to implement the principles asserted in its 2009–2010 National Human Rights Action Plan, and request that the Chinese government implement additional plans to advance human rights and the rule of law.

○ Urge the Chinese government to amend the PRC Criminal Procedure Law to reflect the enhanced rights and protections for lawyers and detained suspects contained in the 2008 revision of the PRC Lawyers Law. Encourage Chinese officials to commit to a specific timetable for revision and implementation of the revised PRC Criminal Procedure Law.

*Introduction*

During the Commission's 2011 reporting year, the Chinese government's failure to uphold legal protections for criminal suspects and defendants, promote transparency of the judicial process, and implement legal reforms highlighted ongoing problems within the criminal justice system. Chinese public security officials continue to contravene international standards by detaining, interrogating, and investigating criminal suspects without adequate due process protections. Closed trial proceedings and unfair trial procedures continue to contravene Chinese and international legal protections and demonstrate the lack of an independent judiciary.

During the year, the Chinese government signaled its resolve to protect what it deemed to be "social stability" through targeted crackdowns on rights advocates and continued reliance on an array of arbitrary and extrajudicial detention measures. In early 2011, Chinese public security officials implemented a harsh crackdown on government critics and rights advocates, including lawyers, bloggers, writers, and democracy activists. In the months that followed, Chinese authorities employed a range of illegal and arbitrary detention measures—including home confinement and enforced disappearances—to "maintain stability" and silence rights advocates. International human rights groups have called the 2011 crackdown one of the most severe in years.

*Abuse of Police Powers: Suppression of Dissent*

During this past year, the Commission observed reports of Chinese law enforcement personnel engaged in a range of abuses targeting human rights advocates, lawyers, writers, and their families.[1] These abuses included harassment, assault, detention, kidnappings, and illegal surveillance.[2] Reported incidents of abuse increased during periods of heightened official sensitivity. Beginning in February 2011, public security officials and plainclothes security personnel detained, harassed, "disappeared," and placed under illegal surveillance prominent rights defenders. The campaign appeared related to official concern over protests in the Middle East and North Africa and to an anonymous online call for so-called "Jasmine" protests within China.[3] By April 18, the non-governmental organization Chinese Human Rights Defenders reported that public security officials had criminally detained 39 rights advocates and that more than 20 individuals remained "disappeared."[4] For example, Chinese police detained Beijing-based lawyer Tang Jitian on February 16 after he attended a meeting to discuss the ongoing "soft detention" of the self-trained legal advocate Chen Guangcheng.[5] Beijing police summoned and detained human rights lawyer and university lecturer Teng Biao on February 19 before searching his residence and confiscating property, including two computers, politically themed books, and documentaries.[6] In February, the Guardian reported that five domestic security protection officers allegedly beat human rights lawyer Liu Shihui after he attempted to attend a planned protest in Guangzhou city, Guangdong province.[7] The Commission also noted increased police abuses against rights defenders and advocates surrounding other politically sensitive events, such as the Nobel Peace

Prize Ceremony in December 2010 and the annual meetings of the National People's Congress and Chinese People's Political Consultative Conference in March 2011.[8] Such arbitrary restrictions on personal liberty, freedom of expression, and freedom of peaceful assembly and association contravene the Universal Declaration of Human Rights and the International Covenant on Civil and Political Rights, as well as China's Constitution and domestic laws.[9]

### Pretrial Detention and Prisons: Torture and Abuse in Custody

Although the Chinese government formally outlawed torture in 1996 with amendments to the PRC Criminal Procedure Law and the PRC Criminal Law,[10] torture and abuse by law enforcement officers remain widespread. In November 2008, the UN Committee against Torture (UNCAT) stated it "remains deeply concerned about the continued allegations . . . of routine and widespread use of torture and ill-treatment of suspects in police custody, especially to extract confessions or information to be used in criminal proceedings."[11] Although China objected to the UNCAT report's findings in its November 2009 followup report, in October 2010, UNCAT submitted a letter to the Chinese government requesting clarification on issues including the legal safeguards to prevent torture, the harassment of lawyers and rights defenders, and the lack of statistical information related to torture.[12]

During this reporting year, the Commission observed multiple reports in which public security officials allegedly employed various torture measures, including beatings, electric shock, cigarette burnings, and sleep deprivation.[13] In January 2011, the Guardian reported on the December 2010 death of local police chief Xie Zhigang in Benxi city, Liaoning province, who reportedly died from a heart attack within a day of his detention. Xie's wife disputed the police account and claimed Xie died as a result of torture, stating, "There were bruises all over [Xie's] body, and deep scars on his wrist and ankles. Five of his ribs were broken."[14] In March 2011, human rights lawyer Zhang Kai released a video of Qian Chengyu, a witness to the murder of village leader and petitioner Qian Yunhui. In the February 2011 video, Qian Chengyu described how public security officials beat him for five hours and deprived him of sleep for thirty hours and explained that the injuries prevented him from standing for a month.[15]

In response to a spate of high-profile suspicious deaths and increased public scrutiny since 2009, Chinese law enforcement agencies reportedly have ordered an overhaul of prisons and detention centers. In 2009 and 2011, Chinese agencies released various guidelines intended to improve oversight responsibilities and enhance supervision of detainees in detention centers.[16] In early 2011, the Ministry of Public Security reportedly delivered a draft revision of the Detention Regulations, the first revision since the Detention Regulations were enacted in 1990.[17] In February 2011, Xinhua reported that in a nationwide campaign to improve oversight of detention centers, prosecutors found 2,207 detention center "bullies" and prosecuted 123 suspected crimes.[18] In a March 2011 China News Weekly interview, Sun Qian, Deputy Procurator-General of the Supreme People's Procuratorate, said that abnormal deaths in recent years had "exposed problems in prison administration law enforcement" and had resulted in reportedly "thorough" official investigations into prisons and detention centers.[19]

### Arrest and Trial Procedure Issues

#### ACCESS TO COUNSEL

The right to legal counsel in criminal trials is not a guaranteed legal right for all defendants in China, even though the PRC Criminal Procedure Law (CPL) and the PRC Lawyers Law provide guidelines for legal representation in criminal trials.[20] Chinese law grants all criminal defendants the right to hire an attorney, but only guarantees legal defense if the defendant is a minor, faces a possible death sentence, or is blind, deaf, or mute. Although the Chinese government has increased funding for legal assistance in recent years, most criminal defendants approach the legal system without access to legal assistance. [For more information on developments in China's legal aid system, see Section III—Access to Justice.] This remains counter to provisions under Article 14(3)(d) of the International Covenant on Civil and Political Rights, which grant the right to defend oneself in person or through legal assistance.[21]

Chinese criminal defendants face two primary obstacles—referred to on occasion as the "two lows" (*liang di*)—in securing criminal defense counsel: The low rate of active representation by lawyers in criminal cases and the low quality of criminal defense.[22] Most Chinese defendants confront the criminal process without the assistance of an attorney.[23] According to a February 2011 Beijing Review article, a professor at China University of Political Science and Law noted that 80 to 90 percent of criminal defendants in China are unable to hire a lawyer.[24] In addition, the higher proportion of risks associated with criminal defense work—as compared with those of civil and commercial work—continues to impact the quality of criminal representation.[25] In recent years, lawyers have been illegally detained, criminally punished, beaten, summoned, and disbarred for performing their legal responsibilities.[26]

Chinese lawyers also remain vulnerable to prosecution under Article 306 of the PRC Criminal Law (commonly referred to as the "lawyer-perjury" statute), a legal provision on evidence fabrication that specifically targets criminal defense attorneys.[27] While harassment of lawyers takes many forms in China, from prosecution for corruption to threats and physical violence, a disproportionately high number of such cases involve charges of evidence fabrication.[28] Many evidence fabrication cases are brought under Article 306, which makes it a crime for defense attorneys or other defense agents to "destroy or forge evidence, help any parties destroy or forge evidence, or coerce or entice witnesses into changing their testimony in defiance of the facts or giving false testimony."[29] Because of the risks presented by Article 306, most defense attorneys reportedly engage in passive defense: they focus on finding flaws and weaknesses in the prosecutors' evidence rather than actively collecting evidence or conducting their own investigations.[30] Chinese criminal defense lawyers acknowledge that the threat of Article 306 of the PRC Criminal Law—also commonly referred to as

"Big Stick 306"—gives prosecutors "unlimited power" to intimidate lawyers and derail criminal defense work.[31]

Specific cases involving Article 306 of the PRC Criminal Law continued to be featured prominently in national Chinese news and in ongoing debates over Article 306. In June 2011, for instance, leading Chinese scholars and lawyers criticized the high profile case against four criminal defense lawyers—Yang Zaixin, Yang Zhonghan, Luo Sifang, and Liang Wucheng—in Beihai city, Guangxi Zhuang Autonomous Region.[32] The four criminal defense attorneys were representing criminal suspect Pei Jinde, accused in a murder trial, when the testimonies of three defense witnesses challenged the prosecution's case.[33] Authorities later detained the four attorneys on suspicion of committing "witness tampering" under Article 306 and arrested the defense witnesses, who were indicted on perjury charges. On June 28, 2011, public security officials formally arrested rights lawyer Yang Zaixin on suspicion of violating Article 306.[34] The three remaining criminal defense lawyers were reportedly released on bail pending trial on suspicion of similar charges.[35] In July 2011, China University of Political Science and Law Professor Chen Guangzhong told Oriental Outlook Magazine that the formal arrest of Yang Zaixin was "wrongful" and that, based on disclosed information, the four lawyers were fulfilling their professional obligations.[36] In July 2011, the Global Times, which operates under the official People's Daily, reported that more than 30 unidentified persons attacked lawyers from Beijing municipality and Shandong and Yunnan provinces who had travelled to Beihai to represent lawyer Yang Zaixin.[37] According to the Global Times article, the assailants reportedly demanded the lawyers not represent client Yang and that they leave immediately.[38]

Chinese legal scholars this past year continued to urge revision of the PRC Criminal Procedure Law, which is reportedly on the National People's Congress agenda, to address the problem of Article 306 and other longstanding issues related to criminal defense counsel. Such longstanding issues include the commonly referred to "three difficulties" (*san nan*) of criminal defense: Gaining access to detained clients, reviewing the prosecutors' case files, and collecting evidence.[39] Although authorities amended the 2008 PRC Lawyers Law to address these issues, inconsistencies between the PRC Lawyers Law and the 1997 PRC Criminal Procedure Law remain. In January 2011, several criminal defense lawyers, interviewed by the Legal Weekly, expressed growing frustrations over limitations within criminal defense work. In addition to the widely discussed "three difficulties," prominent Beijing criminal defense lawyer Xu Lantang raised "ten difficulties"—including the difficulty of getting witnesses to appear in court, the difficulty of getting a hearing for trial on appeal, and the difficulty of participating in the death penalty review process.[40] According to the article, criminal defense lawyers' primary obstacle is having innocence claims accepted by people's courts.[41] A January 2011 Legal Daily article said that the challenges to successfully representing criminal defendants have led to a decline in the rate of legal representation of criminal defendants in China.[42]

FAIRNESS OF CRIMINAL TRIALS

Chinese lawyers and criminal defendants continue to face numerous obstacles in ensuring the application of the right to a fair trial. Although judicial independence is enshrined in the 1997 PRC Criminal Procedure Law, Chinese judges regularly receive political guidance on pending cases, including instructions on how to rule, from both the government and the Communist Party.[43] Closed trials, undue political influence, and a lack of transparency in judicial decisionmaking remain commonplace within the justice system. For criminal suspects that reach the trial stage, the likelihood of a guilty verdict is great. According to 2010 official statistics from the Supreme People's Court, the conviction rate for criminal cases was 98.12 percent.[44] Chinese officials routinely sentence defendants in trials that fall far short of fair trial standards set forth in the International Covenant on Civil and Political Rights.[45]

During this reporting year, the Commission has observed several notable cases in which Chinese judicial authorities failed to provide transparency and uphold defendants' fair trial rights in accordance with domestic and international law. In March 2011, for instance, the Suining Intermediate People's Court in Sichuan province sentenced democracy advocate Liu Xianbin, a signatory to Charter 08 (a treatise advocating political reform and human rights), to 10 years' imprisonment for "inciting subversion of state power."[46] Authorities reportedly denied Liu access to a lawyer for months, which appeared to contravene protections in the PRC Lawyers Law.[47] [For more information about Liu Xianbin, see Section III—Institutions of Democratic Governance.] In August 2011, the Chaoyang District People's Court in Beijing city tried rights advocate Wang Lihong for "creating a disturbance" in connection with her role in organizing a protest outside of a Fujian province courthouse on April 16, 2010.[48] It was not until March 2011, nearly 12 months after the protest, that Chinese authorities criminally detained Wang.[49] At Wang's own trial in August, Wang's criminal defense lawyer, Han Yicun, maintained that the trial was "unfair," since the judge interrupted Wang's final statement and did not permit defense attorney Han to finish his defense statement.[50] In addition, the criminal defense attorneys were unable to photocopy court documents or present arguments before the indictment.[51] In September, the court sentenced Wang to nine months in prison for "creating a disturbance."[52] Additionally, in the past year, the UN Working Group on Arbitrary Detention released Opinion No. 15/2011, which found that the December 2009 criminal case against prominent intellectual Liu Xiaobo "was organized in [a] way which constitutes a breach of fairness."[53]

In June 2010, two regulations took effect that prohibit convictions based on illegally obtained evidence.[54] According to a November 2010 Oriental Outlook Weekly article, however, fewer than 20 percent of lawyers surveyed had used the regulations, and many alleged that the regulations lacked enforceability.[55] In January 2011, a Procuratorial Daily article addressed the reasons behind enforcement obstacles and why the implemented guidelines lack force.[56] The article noted that the evidence regulations "possess their own inherent flaws," "easily result in different interpretations," and suffer from the prejudices of judicial officials.[57]

### *Human Rights Lawyers and Defenders*

Amid a broad crackdown against human rights advocates that began in February 2011, authorities in Beijing municipality and Guangzhou city, Guangdong province, detained at least five prominent human rights lawyers in late February or early March 2011, including Teng Biao, Tang Jitian, Jiang Tianyong, and Tang Jingling.[58] Chinese officials detained other human rights lawyers, such as Li Fangping and Li Xiongbing, for briefer periods in April and May 2011.[59] In at least some instances, authorities required those released to sign "letters of guarantee."[60] According to one unnamed human rights lawyer, the "letters" required that those released guarantee not to commit certain acts, including criticizing the Communist Party, participating in training by overseas organizations, and communicating with overseas organizations.[61] As a result, released human rights lawyers declined to speak to the media about their detentions.[62]

The following are examples from the past year of official mistreatment of Chinese human rights lawyers and defenders.

- In February 2011, security officials in Shandong province reportedly beat self-trained legal advocate Chen Guangcheng and his wife Yuan Weijing. The reported beatings followed the couple's covert recording of video footage in which they described the official surveillance, intimidation, harassment, and abuse their family has endured since Chen's release from prison after serving his full sentence on September 9, 2010.[63]
- In April 2011, Beijing-based human rights lawyer Jin Guanghong disappeared amid a number of apparently politically motivated disappearances.[64] After a Beijing psychiatric hospital reportedly released Jin 10 days later, he was in an "extremely weak physical and mental state."[65] Jin alleged he was beaten and vaguely recalled receiving injections while tied to a bed.[66] He was unable to fully recall the circumstances surrounding his detention.[67] In recent years, Jin had defended a member of the banned Falun Gong spiritual movement in Guangzhou city, Guangdong province, and had participated on the legal defense team in a high-profile 2010 criminal defamation case in Fujian province.[68] [For more information on conditions for Falun Gong practitioners, see Section II—Freedom of Religion—Falun Gong.]
- In April 2011, public security officials in Beijing detained housing rights advocate and former lawyer Ni Yulan on suspicion of "creating a disturbance."[69] The criminal detention of Ni and the disappearance of her husband followed months of police harassment, which included surveillance and disruptions in their electricity, water, and Internet services.[70] Ni is confined to a wheelchair reportedly due to chronic medical conditions and alleged official torture suffered over the past decade.[71]

In 2011, Chinese authorities have continued to pressure human rights lawyers who take on sensitive cases by denying annual professional license renewals during the "annual inspection and assessment process" (*niandu jiancha kaohe*), which justice departments throughout the country completed in July 2011.[72] Lawyers that participate in politically "sensitive" cases—including those involving workers' rights, religious freedom, and political reform—frequently fail to have their professional licenses renewed during the annual assessment.[73] As of mid-July 2011, justice departments failed to renew the professional licenses of at least four human rights lawyers, including Liu Xiaoyuan, Cheng Hai, Li Jinglin, and Li Baiguang.[74] In July 2011, a Caijing article reported that some lawyers viewed the annual assessment system as a "tool to suppress disobedient lawyers."[75] The article claimed that prominent rights lawyer Liu Xiaoyuan failed to pass the 2011 "annual inspection and assessment process" as a result of offending officials.[76] In a subsequent posting on his personal blog, however, Liu denied offending any individuals prior to failing to have his professional license renewed.[77]

The whereabouts and condition of prominent human rights lawyer Gao Zhisheng, who angered Chinese authorities by exposing human rights abuses and representing marginalized citizens and religious practitioners, remain unknown. Weeks after reportedly reappearing publicly in late March 2010, Gao "disappeared" again in mid-April 2010.[78] In January 2011, the Associated Press released information from an April 2010 interview with Gao in which he confirmed being tortured extensively during detention.[79] In February 2011, Freedom Now, a U.S.-based non-governmental organization that represents individual prisoners of conscience, publicly released a November 2010 statement from the UN Working Group on Arbitrary Detention in which the UN agency demanded the Chinese government "proceed to an immediate release of [Gao] and provide for reparation of the harm caused as a result of his situation."[80]

### Arbitrary Detention

Arbitrary detention in China takes many forms and continues to be widely used by Chinese authorities to quell local petitioners, government critics, and rights advocates. Among the forms of arbitrary extralegal and illegal detention are:

- "enforced disappearances";
- "soft detention" (*ruanjin*), a range of extralegal controls under which individuals may be subjected to home confinement, surveillance, restricted movement, and limitations on contact with others;
- reeducation through labor, an administrative detention of up to four years for minor offenses;
- "black jail" (*hei jianyu*) detentions; and
- forcible detention in psychiatric hospitals for non-medical reasons.

"*Shuanggui*," another form of extralegal detention, is used by the Communist Party for investigation of Party members, most often in cases of suspected corruption. The UN Working Group on Arbitrary Detention (UNWGAD) defines the deprivation of personal liberty to be "arbitrary" if it meets one of the following criteria: (1) There is no clear legal basis for the deprivation of liberty; (2) an individual is deprived of his liberty for having exercised rights guaranteed under the Universal Declaration of Human Rights (UDHR) and the International Covenant on Civil and Political Rights (ICCPR); or (3) there is grave non-compliance with fair trial standards set forth in the UDHR and other international human rights instruments.[81] In addition, many forms of arbitrary detention also appear to contravene protections within China's Constitution and domestic laws.[82] In this past year, for example, UNWGAD issued two opinions declaring that the Chinese government's imprisonment of prominent intellectual Liu Xiaobo and house arrest of his wife Liu Xia contravene the UDHR and amount to arbitrary detentions. The opinions call on Chinese officials to immediately release Liu Xiaobo, immediately end Liu Xia's house arrest, and provide reparations to both persons.[83]

### ENFORCED DISAPPEARANCES

During the 2011 reporting year, the Commission observed numerous reported cases of Chinese citizens who went "missing" or "disappeared" into official custody with little or no information about their whereabouts or potential charges against them. In an April 8, 2011, press release, the UN Working Group on Enforced or Involuntary Disappearances (UNWGEID) expressed "serious concern at the recent wave of enforced disappearances that allegedly took place in China over the last few months," adding that it had received "multiple reports of a number of persons having [been] subject to enforced disappearance . . . ."[84] Article 2 of the International Convention for the Protection of All Persons from Enforced Disappearance defines "enforced disappearance" as follows: "the arrest, detention, abduction or any other form of deprivation of liberty by agents of the State or by persons or groups of persons acting with the authorization, support or acquiescence of the State, followed by a refusal to acknowledge the deprivation of liberty or by concealment of the fate or whereabouts of the disappeared person, which place such a person outside the protection of the law."[85] In late May, Chinese Human Rights Defenders reported that at least 22 prominent Chinese rights advocates—including well-known artist and public advocate Ai Weiwei, petitioner Zhou Li, and writer Gu Chuan—had been subjected to enforced disappearances, some for as long as 70 days.[86] In June, UNWGEID issued a press release expressing "serious concern" over all persons subjected to enforced disappearance in China, including the 300 Tibetan monks whom security personnel allegedly removed from Kirti Monastery, Aba county, Aba Tibetan and Qiang Autonomous Prefecture, Sichuan province, on April 21, 2011.[87]

---

### Draft Amendment to the PRC Criminal Procedure Law

In August 2011, the National People's Congress Standing Committee (NPCSC) reviewed a draft amendment to the PRC Criminal Procedure Law (CPL), which includes 99 amendments to the current CPL.[88] Chinese state-run media has reported that any revised draft amendment approved by the NPCSC will likely be deliberated upon and passed by the plenary session of the National People's Congress in March 2012.[89]

According to state-run media reports, legal scholars have said the CPL draft revisions "will help improve the protection of criminal suspects' human rights"[90] and have said the draft amendment complies with international standards.[91] The CPL draft amendment includes revisions that would aim to prohibit forced self-incrimination,[92] and bar collecting evidence obtained through torture.[93] The draft amendment explicitly states that Chinese criminal defense attorneys are not to be monitored when meeting criminal defendants in custody.[94]

International organizations and news media outlets have raised concerns that specific amendment revisions, however, would legalize the current practice of forcibly "disappearing" rights advocates in violation of international standards.[95] The revisions allow Chinese police, in cases involving national security, terrorism, or major instances of bribery, to keep criminal suspects under residential surveillance at a fixed location outside of their homes, with approval from an upper level procuratorate or security organ, for up to six months, if keeping them at their homes would likely "hinder an investigation."[96] The revisions also would permit Chinese police to withhold information about this form of "house arrest" in the case of suspected state security or terrorism cases, if they believed that notifying relatives, as normally required, could "hinder the investigation."[97] Under the International Convention for the Protection of All Persons from Enforced Disappearance, a state commits a crime of enforced disappearance when its agents arrest, detain, abduct, or otherwise deprive a person of liberty and then deny holding the person or conceal the fate or whereabouts of the person.[98] Chinese lawyers and media organizations have also criticized these provisions for having the potential to undermine human rights protections.[99] In September 2011, for instance, an editorial in the official newspaper China Daily acknowledged potential loopholes: "For one thing, the crime of endangering state security is a vague and sprawling conception. Without proper definition and limitations, it is highly vulnerable to abuse. The impossibility of notification and the possibility of impeding investigations are even harder to define and clarify."[100]

---

### "SOFT DETENTION" AND CONTROL

During this reporting year, the Commission noted various reports of law enforcement authorities continuing to use "soft detention" (*ruanjin*) to control and intimidate Chinese citizens.[101] Those under "soft detention" may be subject to various forms of harassment, including home confinement, surveillance, restricted movement, and limited contact with others.[102] The "soft detention" that numerous human rights defenders, advocates, and their family members are subjected to has no basis in Chinese law and constitutes arbitrary detention under international human rights standards.

In the period surrounding the Nobel Peace Prize award ceremony in late 2010, Chinese authorities used "soft detention" measures on more than 100 prominent human rights advocates and associates of 2010 Nobel Peace Prize award recipient Liu Xiaobo.[103] The Commission also noted that in 2011, authorities placed many rights defenders under "soft detention" after releasing them from official custody. The following are some notable "soft detention" cases from the past year:

- From October 2010 to December 2010, state security officials in Wuxi city, Jiangsu province, and Beijing municipality held Ding Zilin, a representative of the Tiananmen Mothers (an advocacy organization of 1989 Tiananmen protest victims' relatives), and her husband Jiang Peikun under "soft detention" for a period of 74 days. The couple was unable to access all forms of communication and unable to contact relatives, friends, and fellow rights advocates.[104]
- In February 2011, a publicly released homemade video of legal advocate Chen Guangcheng showed Chen and his family under "soft detention" in Dongshigu village, Linyi city, Shandong province.[105] Chen and his family have been under "soft detention" since September 2010, when he completed a 51-month sentence for disturbing public order and destroying public property.[106]
- In April 2011, public security officers reportedly placed Jin Tianming, a Protestant pastor, and 500 members of the Shouwang Church in Beijing under "soft detention" after several outdoor worship services organized by the Shouwang Church.[107]

REEDUCATION THROUGH LABOR (RTL)

Public security officers continued to use the reeducation through labor (RTL) system to silence critics and to circumvent the criminal procedure process. RTL is an administrative measure that allows Chinese law enforcement officials to order Chinese citizens, without legal proceedings or due process, to serve a period of administrative detention of up to three years, with the possibility of up to one year extension.[108] While the Bureau of Reeducation Through Labor Administration maintains that the RTL system has been established "to maintain public order, to prevent and reduce crime, and to provide compulsory educational reform to minor offenders,"[109] authorities frequently use RTL to punish, among others, dissidents, drug addicts, petitioners, Falun Gong adherents, and religious practitioners who belong to religious groups not approved by the government.[110]

During this reporting year, the Commission observed numerous accounts of RTL orders violating the legal rights of Chinese citizens, specifically their right to a fair trial and right to be protected from arbitrary detention. In November 2010, an RTL committee in Henan province ordered rights defender Cheng Jianping (who uses the pseudonym Wang Yi) to serve one year of RTL. Authorities alleged that Cheng "disturbed social order" when, in October 2010, she re-tweeted a Twitter message from her fiancé regarding anti-Japanese protests following a fishing incident between China and Japan in disputed waters.[111] The tweet was reportedly satirical in tone and urged demonstrators to protest at the Japanese pavilion at the Shanghai 2010 World Expo.[112] In March 2011, Chinese authorities ordered rights advocate Yang Qiuyu to serve two years of RTL for "creating a disturbance."[113] The RTL order claimed that Yang had "incited" petitioners to go to Tiananmen Square, Wangfujing Street, and other locations in Beijing to cause "trouble."[114] In July 2011, Shanghai authorities released Shanghai petitioner Mao Hengfeng after she served 18 months of RTL for "disturbing the social order."[115] According to her husband Wu Xuewei, Mao was subjected to physical and mental torture while serving her RTL order.[116] After her release, Wu said that Mao, who arrived home in a wheelchair, was unable to speak and did "not have the strength to walk."[117] Mao was initially released on medical parole in February 2011, but officials detained Mao again two days later for unspecified "illegal activities."[118]

Human rights advocates and legal experts in China have been calling for an end to RTL for decades. In August 2010, on the eve of the 53rd anniversary of the establishment of China's RTL system, a number of Chinese scholars, lawyers, and advocates publicly released a "civil rights advocacy letter" calling on the government to immediately abolish the "Decision of the State Council Regarding the Question of Reeducation Through Labor" and other administrative regulations that form the legal basis for RTL.[119] The letter stated that current RTL provisions that permit detention without a judicial trial are unconstitutional and violate Chinese domestic laws and regulations, including the PRC Legislation Law and the PRC Administrative Punishment Law.[120] In February 2011, the advocates reportedly planned to send the signed letter, with over 1,000 signatures, to the National People's Congress Standing Committee.[121]

### "BLACK JAILS": SECRET DETENTION FACILITIES

Chinese authorities continued to use "black jails" (*hei jianyu*)—secret detention sites established by local officials—to detain and punish petitioners who travel to Beijing and provincial capitals to voice complaints and seek redress for injustices.[122] Those detained are denied access to legal counsel and often denied contact with family members or associates.[123] A December 2010 Human Rights Watch report detailed conditions for prisoners in "black jails": "Once detained, petitioners are subjected to abuses including physical and sexual violence, food and sleep deprivation, denial of medical care, and intimidation."[124] [For more information about China's petitioning, or *xinfang* (letters and visits), system, see Section III—Access to Justice.]

In recent years, the Commission has observed reports by international and domestic Chinese media organizations on "black jails," as well as on the network of personnel that intercept and abuse petitioners.[125] In one prominent example of domestic reporting, in September 2010, the Southern Metropolitan Daily reported on a private security company, Anyuanding, which was accused of assisting local governments in abducting and detaining petitioners in "black jails."[126] The New York Times reported in late September 2010 that the "system of interceptors and black jails has flourished in recent years," as Chinese petitioners have sought official redress in the face of illegal land grabs, official misconduct, and other injustices.[127] In April 2011, the Southern Metropolitan Daily reported on the experiences of Sun Yinxia and two individuals forcibly detained in a "black jail" in Sihong county, Jiangsu province, after refusing to sign an agreement allowing the local government to demolish their houses without adequate compensation.[128] Village and township leaders reportedly watched as unidentified guards forcibly detained the "nail household"[129] residents, who reportedly were later "beaten," "sexually harassed," and tortured during their 12 days of detention.[130] According to the article, local residents said that local officials had detained nearly 200 people in the "black jail" since it opened in 2006.[131] In August 2011, Chinese media reported on a "black jail" in Changping district, Beijing municipality, after a petitioner surnamed Zhou revealed information about her four-day detention.[132] According to the Beijing News, several "black jail" "retrievers" forcibly detained Zhou after she visited a local government office in Beijing.[133] The "black jail" personnel reportedly held Zhou and more than 50 detainees in tight quarters without beds, depriving the detainees of their mobile phones and beating some who resisted the detention center management. Zhou said that the detainees, from several provinces, had been forcibly detained or lured into detention.[134]

## SHUANGGUI: EXTRALEGAL INVESTIGATORY DETENTION OF COMMUNIST PARTY MEMBERS

During this reporting year, the Commission continued to observe Chinese media reporting on the Communist Party's use of *shuanggui* (often translated as "double regulation" or "double designation"), a form of extralegal detention that involves summoning Party members under investigation to appear at a designated place at a designated time.[135] Notable cases of high-ranking officials placed under *shuanggui* included: Liu Xiquan, a deputy head of Beijing's Chaoyang district;[136] Zhang Wanqing, Shandong Provincial People's Government Secretary-General;[137] and Zhang Rui, a deputy director at the Department of Exchequer in the Ministry of Finance.[138] *Shuanggui* investigations often precede formal Party disciplinary sanctions or the transfer of suspects to law enforcement agencies if there has been a violation of the criminal law.[139] The investigations at undisclosed locations usually last several months, and officials may extend the investigations for over a year.[140] Those under investigation are "generally held incommunicado and denied some of the protections to which criminal suspects are entitled at least in principle."[141]

---

**Legal Scholar Questions Anti-Crime Campaign's Excesses**

This past year, authorities in Chongqing municipality, Sichuan province, continued a massive, public "anti-crime" sweep (known in Chinese as "striking organized crime and uprooting evil" [*dahei chu'e*]) of criminal syndicates and corrupt officials that netted thousands of arrests and raised various concerns about judicial independence and procedural rights.[142] In an April 2011 public letter, circulated widely, Beijing-based human rights advocate and university professor He Weifang compared the "movement-style" campaign to the turbulent period of the Cultural Revolution.[143] Of the campaign, He writes, "the Cultural Revolution is being replayed, and the ideal of rule of law is right now being lost."[144] He publicly questioned the lack of independent adjudicative and prosecutorial powers and criticized the public security agencies' emphasis on order above all.[145]

---

*Medical Parole*

During this reporting year, Chinese authorities denied medical parole and adequate medical treatment to prisoners, particularly human rights advocates. The U.S. State Department observed in its report on China's human rights situation for 2010 that "[a]dequate, timely medical care for prisoners remained a serious problem, despite official assurances that prisoners have the right to prompt medical treatment."[146] In January 2011, Zeng Jinyan, a rights advocate and the wife of human rights defender Hu Jia, applied for medical parole on behalf of Hu, who suffers from hepatitis and cholelithiasis.[147] As was the case with previous requests, authorities denied the appeal for medical parole, despite Hu's deteriorating condition.[148] The Commission noted at least one case where untimely medical parole release had likely contributed to a decline in a prisoner's medical condition. In December 2010, rights advocate Zhang Jianhong, who wrote under the pen name Li Hong, died after being released on medical parole on June 5, 2010.[149] Authorities had repeatedly denied Zhang medical parole, which resulted in an apparent worsening of his condition.[150]

In addition, authorities appeared to use medical parole as a measure to silence rights advocates and defenders. In December 2010, authorities released rights advocate Zhao Lianhai, the head of an advocacy group for parents of children sickened by melamine-tainted milk, on medical parole.[151] Some supporters, however, feared that Zhao's release was intended to keep him silent.[152] In April 2010, Zhao reportedly broke this public silence to comment on the broad crackdown on rights advocates and to detail the intense pressure he and his family were living under.[153] Police reportedly then threatened to rescind Zhao's medical parole if he continued to comment on the treatment of human rights advocates.[154] In February 2011, Shanghai authorities terminated the medical parole release of Shanghai petitioner Mao Hengfeng, two days after her release from a reeducation through labor (RTL) center.[155] Although authorities cited "illegal activities inconsistent with [the stipulations of] medical parole" as the rationale, they reportedly did not specify the alleged "illegal activities."[156] Mao reportedly suffered torture and ill treatment throughout her RTL detention.[157]

*Capital Punishment*

During this reporting year, the Chinese government maintained its policy of not releasing details on the thousands of prisoners reportedly executed annually and continued to keep information on the death penalty a state secret. Chinese officials also maintained the stated goal of limiting the number of executions. In March 2011, for instance, Supreme People's Court (SPC) President Wang Shengjun emphasized the state policy of "strictly controlling and carefully applying the death penalty" and urged "improving the death penalty review process" in his report to the annual session of the National People's Congress.[158] In May 2011, the SPC stated in its annual 2010 work report that courts should suspend death sentences for two years, if the criminal circumstances do not require an "immediate execution."[159] On February 25, 2011, the National People's Congress Standing Committee (NPCSC) passed the eighth amendment to the PRC Criminal Law, which reduced the number of crimes punishable by the death penalty from 68 to 55.[160] As the revision was the first time the Chinese legislature reduced the number of crimes subject to capital punishment since enacting the PRC Criminal Law in 1979, the country's official media heralded the reform as a step "to restructure its penalty system and better protect human rights."[161] In an August 2010 Southern Weekend article on the then proposed amendment, a member of the National People's Congress Legal Committee pointed out that authorities rarely, if ever, applied the death penalty for the 13 crimes under consideration for reclassification as non-capital offenses.[162]

# Endnotes

[1] Chinese Human Rights Defenders, "Twenty-Two Years After Tiananmen Massacre, Worst Repression in a Generation," 2 June 11; Tania Branigan, "Crackdown in China Spreads Terror Among Dissidents," Guardian, 31 March 11.

[2] Chinese Human Rights Defenders, "U.S. Must Voice Concerns Over China's Assault on Human Rights Lawyers During the Upcoming Legal Experts Dialogue With China," 7 June 11; "China Cracking Down on Rights Lawyers: Amnesty," Agence France-Presse, 29 June 11; Andrew Jacobs and Jonathan Ansfield, "China's Intimidation of Dissidents Said To Persist After Prison," New York Times, 17 February 11.

[3] "Authorities Crack Down on Rights Defenders, Lawyers, Artists, Bloggers," Congressional-Executive Commission on China, 3 May 11.

[4] Chinese Human Rights Defenders, "Individuals Affected by the Crackdown Following Call for 'Jasmine Revolution,'" 18 April 11.

[5] Tania Branigan, "Fears Grow After Chinese Human Rights Lawyer Detained," Guardian, 18 February 11.

[6] Human Rights in China, "Lawyers and Activists Detained, Summoned, and Harassed in 'Jasmine Rallies' Crackdown," 23 February 11; "China Releases Detained Activist," New York Times, 29 April 11.

[7] Tania Branigan, "Chinese Lawyer Beaten Ahead of Jasmine Revolution Protests," Guardian, 21 February 11.

[8] Chinese Human Rights Defenders, "Chinese Reactions to Liu Xiaobo's Nobel Peace Prize—From Both Sides," 3 January 11; Human Rights in China, "Lawyers and Activists Detained, Summoned, and Harassed in 'Jasmine Rallies' Crackdown," 23 February 11.

[9] Universal Declaration of Human Rights, adopted and proclaimed by UN General Assembly resolution 217 A (III) of 10 December 48, arts. 3, 5, 9, 19, 20 [hereinafter UDHR]; International Covenant on Civil and Political Rights, adopted by UN General Assembly resolution 2200A (XXI) of 16 December 66, entry into force 23 March 76, arts. 7, 9(1), 19(1), 19(2), 21, 22(1) [hereinafter ICCPR]; PRC Constitution, enacted and effective 4 December 82, amended 12 April 88, 29 March 93, 15 March 99, 14 March 04, arts. 35 (freedom of speech, press, assembly), 37 (freedom of person), 41 (right to criticize state organ or functionary).

[10] PRC Criminal Law [Zhonghua renmin gongheguo xingfa], enacted 1 July 79, amended 14 March 97, effective 1 October 97, amended 25 December 99, 31 August 01, 29 December 01, 28 December 02, 28 February 05, 29 June 06, 28 February 09, 25 February 11, arts. 247, 248; PRC Criminal Procedure Law [Zhonghua renmin gongheguo xingshi susong fa], enacted 1 July 79, amended 17 March 96, effective 1 January 97, art. 43.

[11] UN Committee against Torture, 41st Session, Consideration of Reports Submitted by State Parties Under Article 19 of the Convention: Concluding Observations of the Committee against Torture—China, CAT/C/CHN/CO/4, 12 December 08, para. 11.

[12] UN Committee against Torture, "Request for Further Clarification," 29 October 10.

[13] See, e.g., "Chinese Dissident Writer, Freed After 5 Years in Jail, Says Treatment Was 'Beyond Imagination,'" Associated Press, reprinted in Washington Post, 14 September 11; Peter Foster, "Chinese Dissidents Describe Physical and Mental Torture at Hands of Regime," Telegraph, 14 September 11; "Missing China Dissident Recounted Abuse," Agence France-Presse, reprinted in Taipei Times, 12 January 11; Tania Branigan, "Chief's Widow Alleges Torture After He Dies in Custody," Guardian, 14 January 11; "Benxi City 'Xie Zhigang Incident' Interview With the Joint Investigation Team Leader" [Benxi shi "xiezhigang shijian" lianhe diaocha zu fuze ren jieshou jizhe caifang], Northeast News, 13 January 11; Tania Branigan, "Chinese Activists Seized in Human Rights Crackdown Accuse Authorities of Torture," Guardian, 13 September 11; Jiang Li, "State Tax Cadre 'Commits Suicide' in Prison; Prison Refuses to Accept Responsibility" [Guoshui ganbu jianyu zhong "bei zisha," jianyu ju bu chengdan zeren], Boxun, 25 January 11.

[14] Tania Branigan, "Chief's Widow Alleges Torture After He Dies in Custody," Guardian, 14 January 11; "Benxi City 'Xie Zhigang Incident' Interview With the Joint Investigation Team Leader" [Benxi shi "xie zhigang shijian" lianhe diaocha zu fuze ren jieshou jizhe caifang], Northeast News, 13 January 11.

[15] Yan Jianbiao, "'Yueqing Case' Witness Suffers Torture To Extract Confession" ["Yueqing an" zhengren zhi zao xingxun bigong], Caijing, 24 March 11.

[16] Wang Quanbao, "SPP Sun Qian, Deputy Procurator General: Do Not Allow Unexpected Deaths in the Detention Centers" [Zuigao jian fu jiancha zhang sun qian: bu yunxu kanshousuo chuxian yiwai siwang], China News Weekly, reprinted in Sina, 10 March 11.

[17] Wang Lina, "'Detention Regulations' Draft Revision Submitted: To Respect Prisoners as Human" ["Kanshousuo tiaoli" xiuding cao'an yi shangbao: ba fanren dang ren lai zunzhong], China Youth On line, 9 March 11.

[18] "China Pushes Forward Judicial Reform by Enhancing Supervision, Person-Centered Care," Xinhua, 20 February 11.

[19] Wang Quanbao, "SPP Sun Qian, Deputy Procurator General: Do Not Allow Unexpected Deaths in the Detention Centers" [Zuigao jian fu jiancha zhang sun qian: bu yunxu kanshousuo chuxian yiwai siwang], China News Weekly, reprinted in Sina, 10 March 11.

[20] According to Article 34 of the PRC Criminal Procedure Law, the court "shall designate a lawyer that is obligated to provide legal aid to serve as a defender" if the defendant does not have a lawyer and is blind, deaf, mute, a minor, or facing the possibility of a death sentence. In cases in which the criminal defendant "has not entrusted anyone to be his defender due to financial difficulties or other reasons, the People's Court may designate a lawyer that is obligated to provide legal aid to serve as a defender." Article 42 of the PRC Law on Lawyers states that lawyers must fulfill their obligations to provide legal aid services. For more information see the texts: PRC Criminal Procedure Law [Zhonghua renmin gongheguo xingshi susong fa],

enacted 1 July 79, amended 17 March 96, effective 1 January 97, art. 34; PRC Lawyers Law [Zhonghua renmin gongheguo lushi fa], enacted 15 May 96, amended 29 December 01, revised 28 October 07, effective 1 June 08, art. 42.

[21] International Covenant on Civil and Political Rights, adopted by UN General Assembly resolution 2200A (XXI) of 16 December 66, entry into force 23 March 76.

[22] Zhang Youyi, "High Risks Result in Low Defense Rates, Criminal Defense Lawyers Face Six Problems" [Gao fengxian zhishi bianhu lu di xingshi bianhu lushi mianlin liu nanti], Legal Daily, reprinted in Xinhua, 6 January 08.

[23] Bureau of Democracy, Human Rights, and Labor, U.S. Department of State, Country Report on Human Rights Practices—2009, China (includes Tibet, Hong Kong, and Macau), 11 March 10.

[24] Yuan Yuan, "Aiding in Defense," Beijing Review, 6 February 11.

[25] Zhang Youyi, "High Risks Result in Low Defense Rates, Criminal Defense Lawyers Face Six Problems" [Gao fengxian zhishi bianhu lu di xingshi bianhu lushi mianlin liu nanti], Legal Daily, reprinted in Xinhua, 6 January 08.

[26] Amnesty International, "Against the Law: Crackdown on China's Human Rights Lawyers Deepens," June 2011, 3, 24–27, 45–50; Paul Mooney, "Silence of the Chinese Dissidents," South China Morning Post, 4 July 11; Zhang Youyi, "High Risks Result in Low Defense Rates, Criminal Defense Lawyers Face Six Problems" [Gao fengxian zhishi bianhu lu di xingshi bianhu lushi mianlin liu nanti], Legal Daily, reprinted in Xinhua, 6 January 08.

[27] Patrick Kar-wai Poon, China Human Rights Lawyers Concern Group, "Rights Defense Lawyers and the Rule of Law in China," 18 May 11. For CECC analysis on Article 306, see, e.g., "Defense Lawyers Turned Defendants: Zhang Jianzhong and the Criminal Prosecution of Defense Lawyers in China," Congressional-Executive Commission on China, 27 May 03.

[28] Yanfei Ran, "When Chinese Criminal Defense Lawyers Become the Criminals," Fordham International Law Journal, Vol. 32, Issue 3 (2008), 988, 1023; "'Big Stick 306' and China's Contempt for the Law," New York Times, 5 May 11.

[29] PRC Criminal Law [Zhonghua renmin gongheguo xingfa], enacted 1 July 79, amended 14 March 97, effective 1 October 97, amended 25 December 99, 31 August 01, 29 December 01, 28 December 02, 28 February 05, 29 June 06, 28 February 09, 25 February 11, art. 306.

[30] "Ignoring Facts and Law as a Concession to Popular Will Actually Contravenes the Will of the People" ["Weile qianjiu minyi bugu shishi he falu cai shi zhenzheng weibei minyi"], China Youth Daily, 18 June 09. For more information about Article 306, see CECC, 2010 Annual Report, 10 October 10, 90.

[31] "'Big Stick 306' and China's Contempt for the Law," New York Times, 5 May 11.

[32] Human Rights in China, "Guangxi Rights Defense Lawyer Yang Zaixin Formally Arrested," 5 July 11.

[33] Ibid.; Li Jiayu, "Mob Storms Into Hotel, Beats Up Two Defense Lawyers," Global Times, 20 July 11.

[34] Human Rights in China, "Guangxi Rights Defense Lawyer Yang Zaixin Formally Arrested," 5 July 11.

[35] Chinese Human Rights Defenders, "China Human Rights Briefing June 29–July 6, 2011," 6 July 11; Human Rights in China, "Guangxi Rights Defense Lawyer Yang Zaixin Formally Arrested," 5 July 11.

[36] Chen Guangzhong, "I Think Arresting These Four Lawyers Is Wrong" ["Wo renwei zhua zhe si ming lushi shi cuowu de"], Oriental Outlook, July 2011.

[37] Li Jiayu, "Mob Storms Into Hotel, Beats Up Two Defense Lawyers," Global Times, 20 July 11. For more information on the assault, see "Lawyers Group Representing Yang Zaixin Attacked and Unable To Work" [Yang zaixin daibiao lushi tuan zao weigong wufa gongzuo], Radio Free Asia, 19 July 11.

[38] Li Jiayu, "Mob Storms Into Hotel, Beats Up Two Defense Lawyers," Global Times, 20 July 11.

[39] Sun Jibin, "How 'Three Difficulties' of Criminal Defense Became '10 Difficulties'" [Xingshi bianhu "san nan" weihe bian "shi nan"], Legal Weekly, 20 January 11; "'Big Stick 306' and China's Contempt for the Law," New York Times, 5 May 11.

[40] Sun Jibin, "How 'Three Difficulties' of Criminal Defense Became '10 Difficulties'" [Xingshi bianhu "san nan" weihe bian "shi nan"], Legal Weekly, 20 January 11; Dui Hua Foundation "Translation: How 'Three Difficulties' of Criminal Defense Became '10 Difficulties,'" 2 February 11.

[41] Sun Jibin, "How 'Three Difficulties' of Criminal Defense Became '10 Difficulties'" [Xingshi bianhu "san nan" weihe bian "shi nan"], Legal Weekly, 20 January 11.

[42] Ibid.

[43] Bureau of Democracy, Human Rights, and Labor, U.S. Department of State, "Country Report on Human Rights Practices—2010 Human Rights Report: China (includes Tibet, Hong Kong, and Macau)," 8 April 11.

[44] Supreme People's Court,"Table on Circumstances for Accused in 2010 China Court Criminal Case Judgments" [2010 Nian quanguo fayuan shenli xingshi anjian beigao ren panjue shengxiao qingkuang biao], 24 March 11. According to official 2010 criminal adjudication statistics, Chinese authorities approved 999 individual acquittals and 17,957 exemptions from criminal punishment. Chinese authorities imposed criminal penalties on 1,007,419 criminal defendants.

[45] International Covenant on Civil and Political Rights, adopted by UN General Assembly resolution 2200A (XXI) of 16 December 66, entry into force 23 March 76.

[46] Andrew Jacobs, "Chinese Democracy Advocate Is Sentenced to 10 Years," New York Times, 25 March 11; Human Rights in China, "Activist Sentenced to Ten Years for Inciting Subversion; Essays Cited as Evidence," 25 March 11; Chinese Human Rights Defenders, "Liu Xianbin Case Trial Oral Judgment Announcement of 10 Years, Family and Lawyers Cannot Visit" [Liu xianbin an fating koutou xuanpan shi nian xingqi, jiaren lushi wufa huijian], 25 March 11;

Gillian Wong, "China Sentences Democracy Activist to 10 Years," Associated Press, reprinted in Yahoo!, 25 March 11.

[47] Andrew Jacobs, "Chinese Democracy Advocate Is Sentenced to 10 Years," New York Times, 25 March 11.

[48] Chinese Human Rights Defenders, "China Human Rights Briefing August 10–15, 2011," 16 August 11; Human Rights in China, "Lawyers Report Procedural Irregularities at Trial of Rights Activist Wang Lihong," 13 August 11.

[49] Peter Foster, "Chinese Internet-Activist on Trial," Telegraph, 12 August 11; "Chinese Citizens Support Jailed Activist Wang Lihong," New Tang Dynasty Television, 9 August 11.

[50] Human Rights in China, "Rights Defender Wang Lihong Sentenced to Nine Months," 9 September 11; Peter Foster, "Chinese Internet-Activist on Trial," Telegraph, 12 August 11; Human Rights in China, "Lawyers Report Procedural Irregularities at Trial of Rights Activist Wang Lihong," 13 August 11; "Wang Lihong's 'Creating a Disturbance' Lawyer Denounces Unfair Trial" [Wang lihong "zishi an" lushi chi tingshen bugong], BBC, 12 August 11.

[51] Chinese Human Rights Defenders, "China Human Rights Briefing August 10–15, 2011," 16 August 11; Peter Foster, "Chinese Internet-Activist on Trial," Telegraph, 12 August 11; "Wang Lihong's 'Creating a Disturbance' Lawyer Denounces Unfair Trial" [Wang lihong "zishi an" lushi chi tingshen bugong], BBC, 12 August 11.

[52] Human Rights in China, "Lawyers Report Procedural Irregularities at Trial of Rights Activist Wang Lihong," 13 August 11; Human Rights in China, "Rights Defender Wang Lihong Sentenced to Nine Months," 9 September 11.

[53] Freedom Now, "UN Declares Detention of Imprisoned Nobel Peace Prize Laureate and Wife Illegal; Calls for Immediate Release," 1 August 11.

[54] Supreme People's Court, Supreme People's Procuratorate, Ministry of Public Security, Ministry of State Security, and Ministry of Justice Circular Regarding the Issue of "Provisions Concerning Questions About Examining and Judging Evidence in Death Penalty Cases" and "Provisions Concerning Questions About Exclusion of Illegal Evidence in Handling Criminal Cases" [Zuigao renmin fayuan zuigao renmin jiancha yuan gongan bu guojia anquan bu sifa bu yinfa "guanyu banli sixing anjian shencha panduan zhengju ruogan wenti de guiding" he "guanyu banli xingshi anjian paichu feifa zhengju ruogan wenti de guiding" de tongzhi], issued 13 June 10; Provisions Concerning Questions About Exclusion of Illegal Evidence in Handling Criminal Cases [Guanyu banli xingshi anjian paichu feifa zhengju ruogan wenti de guiding], effective 1 July 10, arts. 1, 7; Provisions Concerning Questions About Examining and Judging Evidence in Death Penalty Cases [Guanyu banli sixing anjian shencha panduan zhengju ruogan wenti de guiding], effective 1 July 10, arts. 18(4), 19, 34; Yang Ming and Zhang Hailin, "Staggered Start to 'Illegal Evidence Exclusion'" [Feifa "zhengju paichu" panshan qibu], Oriental Outlook Weekly, November 2011.

[55] Yang Ming and Zhang Hailin, "Staggered Start to 'Illegal Evidence Exclusion'" [Feifa "zhengju paichu" panshan qibu], Oriental Outlook Weekly, November 2011.

[56] Li Guomin, "Why the Illegal Evidence Exclusionary Regulations Cannot Be Strictly Enforced" [Feifa zhengju paichu guize weihe buneng yange zhixing], Procuratorial Daily, 10 January 11.

[57] Ibid.

[58] Edward Wong, "Human Rights Advocates Vanish as China Intensifies Crackdown," New York Times, 11 March 11.

[59] "China Frees Rights Lawyer but Another Disappears," Agence France-Presse, reprinted in Google, 5 May 11.

[60] "Human Rights Lawyers Suppressed in Different Ways" [Weiquan lushi shou butong xingshi daya], Radio Free Asia, 26 May 11; "Friend Says Chinese Civil Rights Lawyer Resurfaces," Associated Press, reprinted in Google, 4 May 11; Chris Buckley, "China Dissident Released After U.S. Official's Visit," Reuters, 29 April 11.

[61] "Human Rights Lawyers Suppressed in Different Ways" [Weiquan lushi shou butong xingshi daya], Radio Free Asia, 26 May 11.

[62] Ibid.; "Friend Says Chinese Civil Rights Lawyer Resurfaces," Associated Press, reprinted in Google, 4 May 11; Chris Buckley, "China Dissident Released After U.S. Official's Visit," Reuters, 29 April 11.

[63] ChinaAid, "Urgent! Chen and Wife Beaten Severely, Chinese Citizens Appeal to America," 10 February 11; Ding Xiao, "Blind Activist, Wife Beaten," Radio Free Asia, 11 February 11; ChinaAid, "Detained Blind Activist Chen Guangcheng's Wife Reveals Details of Torture," 16 June 11. For CECC analysis, see "Chen Guangcheng, Wife Reportedly Beaten After Release of Video Detailing Official Abuse," 11 March 11.

[64] John Zhang, "The Silencing of China's Human Rights Lawyers," Epoch Times, 3 March 11.

[65] Rona Rui, "Beijing Rights Lawyer Suffers Memory Loss After Ten-Day Detention," Epoch Times, 27 April 11; Chinese Human Rights Defenders, "Lawyer Jin Guanghong Tortured, Cannot Remember the Facts Surrounding His Disappearance," 23 April 11.

[66] Clear Harmony, "Lawyer Jin Guanghong Persecuted and Now Suffering From Partial Amnesia," 21 May 11.

[67] Rona Rui, "Beijing Rights Lawyer Suffers Memory Loss After Ten-Day Detention," Epoch Times, 27 April 11; Chinese Human Rights Defenders, "Lawyer Jin Guanghong Tortured, Cannot Remember the Facts Surrounding His Disappearance," 23 April 11.

[68] "Concern Over Rights Lawyer," Radio Free Asia, 13 April 11.

[69] Feng Weimin, Chinese Human Rights Defenders, "Beijing Human Rights Lawyer Ni Yulan Criminally Detained" [Beijing weiquan lushi ni yulan bei xingshi juliu], 14 April 11.

[70] Chinese Human Rights Defenders, "Activist Ni Yulan Becomes Latest Victim of 'Jasmine' Crackdown," 14 April 11.

[71] Ibid.

[72] For CECC analysis, see "Authorities Deny Human Rights Lawyers Professional License Renewals," Congressional-Executive Commission on China, 10 December 10.

[73] China Human Rights Lawyers Concern Group, "Four Human Rights Lawyers Barred From Passing the Annual Assessment," 19 July 11; Aizhixing, "Aizhixing Strongly Concerned That Many Lawyers Still Have Not Passed Annual Assessment for Professional Lawyers" [Ai zhi xing qianglie guanzhu duo ming lushi shangwei tongguo lushi zhiye niandu kaohe], reprinted in Boxun, 28 June 11.

[74] China Human Rights Lawyers Concern Group, "Four Human Rights Lawyers Barred From Passing the Annual Assessment," 19 July 11.

[75] Xu Kai, "'Chinese Characteristics' of Lawyers Association" ["Zhongguo tese" de luxie], Caijing Magazine, 18 July 11.

[76] Ibid.

[77] Liu Xiaoyuan, "'Chinese Characteristics' of Lawyers Association" ["Zhongguo tese" de luxie], Liu Xiaoyuan's Blog, reprinted in Sina, 19 July 11.

[78] "Chinese Human Rights Defender Gao Zhisheng Disappears Again," CECC China Human Rights and Rule of Law Update, No. 5, 4 June 10, 2.

[79] Charles Hutzler, "AP Exclusive: Missing Chinese Lawyer Told of Abuse," Associated Press, reprinted in Bloomberg, 10 January 11.

[80] Edward Wong, "U.N. Rights Group Calls on China To Release Lawyer," New York Times, 28 March 11; Office of the UN High Commissioner for Human Rights, Working Group on Arbitrary Detention, Opinion No. 26/2010 (People's Republic of China), reprinted in Freedom Now, 6 July 10.

[81] Office of the UN High Commissioner for Human Rights, Working Group on Arbitrary Detention, Fact Sheet No. 26, May 2000, sec. IV; International Covenant on Civil and Political Rights (ICCPR), adopted by UN General Assembly resolution 2200A (XXI) of 16 December 66, entry into force 23 March 76, arts. 12, 18, 19, 21, 22, 25, 26, and 27; Universal Declaration of Human Rights, adopted and proclaimed by UN General Assembly resolution 217A (III) of 10 December 48, arts. 7, 10, 13, 14, 18, 19, and 21. The ICCPR provides that the deprivation of an individual's liberty is permissible only "on such grounds and in accordance with such procedure as are established by law," and that an individual must be promptly informed of the reasons for his detention and any charges against him or her. See ICCPR, arts. 9(1), 9(2).

[82] See, e.g., PRC Constitution, enacted and effective 4 December 82, amended 12 April 88, 29 March 93, 15 March 99, 14 March 04, arts. 35, 37, 41; PRC Criminal Procedure Law [Zhonghua renmin gongheguo xingshi susong fa], enacted 1 July 79, amended 17 March 96, effective 1 January 97, art. 3; PRC Public Security Administration Punishment Law [Zhonghua renmin gongheguo zhian guanli chufa fa], enacted 28 August 05, effective 1 March 06, arts. 3, 9, 10, 16; PRC Legislation Law [Zhonghua renmin gongheguo lifa fa], enacted 15 March 00, effective 1 July 00, art. 8(v).

[83] Freedom Now, "UN Declares Detention of Imprisoned Nobel Peace Prize Laureate and Wife Illegal; Calls for Immediate Release," 1 August 11; "UN Group Calls for Immediate Release of Liu Xiaobo and Wife Liu Xia," Congressional-Executive Commission on China, 12 August 11.

[84] Office of the UN High Commissioner for Human Rights, "China: UN Expert Body Concerned About Recent Wave of Enforced Disappearances," 8 April 11.

[85] International Convention for the Protection of All Persons From Enforced Disappearance, adopted by UN General Assembly resolution A/RES/61/177 of 20 December 06, entry into force 23 December 10, art. 2.

[86] Chinese Human Rights Defenders, "Individuals Affected by the Crackdown Following Call for 'Jasmine Revolution,'" 30 May 11.

[87] Office of the UN High Commissioner for Human Rights, "China: UN Expert Body Seriously Concerned About Tibetan Monks Reportedly Subjected to Enforced Disappearance," 8 June 11. For more information, see "After Monk's Suicide: Coerced Removal and 'Education' for Monks; Possible Murder Charges," Congressional-Executive Commission on China, 17 August 11.

[88] "China To Amend Criminal Procedural Law," Xinhua, reprinted in China Daily, 24 August 11; National People's Congress, "Criminal Procedure Law Amendments (Draft): Explanation of Provisions and Draft" [Xingshi susongfa xiuzheng'an (cao'an) tiaowen ji cao'an shuoming], 30 August 11; PRC Criminal Procedure Law [Zhonghua renmin gongheguo xingshi susongfa], enacted 1 July 79, amended 17 March 96, effective 1 January 97. For more information on reviews of draft laws, see Article 27 of the PRC Legislation Law [Zhonghua renmin gongheguo lifafa], issued 15 March 00, effective 1 July 00, art. 27.

[89] "Procedural Justice," China Daily, 25 August 11.

[90] "China To Amend Criminal Procedural Law To Prevent Forced Confessions," Xinhua, 24 August 11.

[91] "China's Draft Law Amendment in Conformity With International Conventions: Experts," Xinhua, 30 August 11.

[92] National People's Congress, "Criminal Procedure Law Amendments (Draft): Explanation of Provisions and Draft" [Xingshi susongfa xiuzheng'an (cao'an) tiaowen ji cao'an shuoming], 30 August 11, item 14; PRC Criminal Procedure Law [Zhonghua renmin gongheguo xingshi susongfa], enacted 1 July 79, amended 17 March 96, effective 1 January 97, art. 43.

[93] National People's Congress, "Criminal Procedure Law Amendments (Draft): Explanation of Provisions and Draft" [Xingshi susongfa xiuzheng'an (cao'an) tiaowen ji cao'an shuoming], 30 August 11, item 17.

[94] Ibid., item 7; PRC Criminal Procedure Law [Zhonghua renmin gongheguo xingshi susongfa], enacted 1 July 79, amended 17 March 96, effective 1 January 97, art. 36.

[95] For more information on the international organizations and experts' criticism of the draft amendment's treatment of residential surveillance, see, e.g., Human Rights Watch, "China: Don't Legalize Secret Detention," 1 September 11; Michael Wines, "More Chinese Dissidents Appear to Disappear," New York Times, 2 September 11; Jaime FlorCruz, "Proposed Legal Changes in China Cause Jitters," CNN, 3 September 11.

[96] National People's Congress, "Criminal Procedure Law Amendments (Draft): Explanation of Provisions and Draft" [Xingshi susongfa xiuzheng'an (cao'an) tiaowen ji cao'an shuoming], 30 August 11, item 30.

[97] Ibid.

[98] International Convention for the Protection of All Persons From Enforced Disappearance, adopted by UN General Assembly resolution A/RES/61/177 of 12 January 07, entry in force 23 December 10, item 2.

[99] See, e.g., Michael Wines, "More Chinese Dissidents Appear To Disappear," New York Times, 2 September 11; Jaime FlorCruz, "Proposed Legal Changes in China Cause Jitters," CNN, 3 September 11; "Amend Legal Procedures," China Daily, 1 September 11.

[100] "Amend Legal Procedures," China Daily, 1 September 11.

[101] Human Rights Watch, "China: Free Unlawfully Detained Legal Activists, Relatives," 22 February 11; Didi Kirsten Tatlow, "Out of Jail in China, but Not Free," New York Times, 9 March 11; Chinese Human Rights Defenders, "Elections Expert Yao Lifa Abused and Beaten During Soft Detention Period," reprinted in Boxun, 13 December 10.

[102] Human Rights Watch, "China: Free Unlawfully Detained Legal Activists, Relatives," 22 February 11; Didi Kirsten Tatlow, "Out of Jail in China, but Not Free," New York Times, 9 March 11; "China Nobel Laureate Wife Fears Going 'Crazy': Activists," Agence France-Presse, reprinted in Google, 26 February 11.

[103] Chinese Human Rights Defenders, "Chinese Reactions to Liu Xiaobo's Nobel Peace Prize—From Both Sides," 3 January 11.

[104] Human Rights in China, "Prominent Rights Activists Detail Life in 74-Day House Arrest," 30 December 10.

[105] Andrew Jacobs and Jonathan Ansfield, "China's Intimidation of Dissidents Said To Persist After Prison," New York Times, 17 February 11.

[106] Michael Wines, "A Chinese Advocate Is Freed, but Stays Under Surveillance," New York Times, 9 September 10; Ian Johnson and Jonathan Ansfield, "Chinese Officials Beat Activist and His Wife, Group Says," New York Times, 17 June 11.

[107] Andrew Jacobs, "China Detains Church Members at Easter Services," New York Times, 24 April 11.

[108] CECC, 2007 Annual Report, 10 October 07, 39–41; Dui Hua Foundation, "Reference Materials on China's Criminal Justice System, Vol. 2 (June 2009), iv; CECC, 2008 Annual Report, 31 October 08, 36–37; Chinese Human Rights Defenders, "Re-Education Through Labor Abuses Continue Unabated: Overhaul Long Overdue," 4 February 09, 4.

[109] Bureau of Reeducation Through Labor Administration, "A Brief Description of China's Reeducation Through Labor System" [Zhongguo laodong jiaoyang zhidu jianjie], accessed 14 July 11.

[110] Xiaobing Li, Civil Liberties in China, (Santa Barbara, California: ABC–CLIO, 2010), 118; Human Rights in China, "Reeducation Through Labor: A Summary of Regulatory Issues and Concerns," 1 February 01; Jim Yardley, "Issue in China: Many in Jails Without Trial," New York Times, 9 May 05; Chinese Human Rights Defenders, "Re-Education Through Labor Abuses Continue Unabated: Overhaul Long Overdue," 4 February 09, 3.

[111] "News Update: Rights Advocate Wang Yi (Cheng Jianping) Ordered To Serve One Year of Reeducation Through Labor" [Kuaixun: Weiquan renshi wang yi (cheng jianping) bei laojiao yi nian], Boxun, 15 November 10; Human Rights in China, "Lawyers Appeal to Twitter CEO for Help," 9 January 11.

[112] Chinese Human Rights Defenders, "Update: Human Rights Defender Wang Yi Sent to RTL" [Kuaixun: weiquan renshi wang yi zheng yao bei song qu laojiao], reprinted in Boxun, 15 November 10.

[113] Human Rights in China, "Two Years of Reeducation-Through-Labor for Rights Activist Yang Qiuyu," 14 April 11.

[114] Ibid.

[115] "China: Mao Hengfeng Released From Prison in a Wheelchair," Asia News, reprinted in Spero News, 30 July 11.

[116] Ibid.

[117] Human Rights in China, "Petitioner Mao Hengfeng Released From Reeducation-Through-Labor in Serious Condition," 28 July 11.

[118] "China: Mao Hengfeng Released From Prison in a Wheelchair," Asia News, reprinted in Spero News, 30 July 11; Human Rights in China, "Petitioner Mao Hengfeng Released From Reeducation-Through-Labor in Serious Condition," 28 July 11.

[119] Hai Yan, "Thousands of Chinese Citizens Jointly Sign Letter To Abolish Reeducation Through Labor System" [Zhongguo qian gongmin lian shu yaoqiu feichu laojiao zhidu], Voice of America, 16 February 11.

[120] Ibid.

[121] Ibid.

[122] Liu Chang, "Controversy Over 'Black Jails' Continues," Global Times, 4 May 11; "Campaigner Detained in Beijing," Radio Free Asia, 2 February 11; Chris Buckley, "China's Wen Meets Petitioners in Show of Worry Over Discontent," Reuters, 25 January 11.

[123] Human Rights Watch, "An Alleyway in Hell: China's Abusive 'Black Jails,'" 12 November 09.

[124] Human Rights Watch, "Closing China's Network of Secret Jails," 9 December 10.

[125] See, e.g., Chinese Human Rights Defenders, "Jilin Petitioner Qu Yanjiang Is Tricked Back Into Black Jail Custody by Retrievers" [Jilin fang min qu yanjiang bei jie fang ren pian hui guan hei jianyu], reprinted in Boxun, 24 October 10; Gan Hao, "Petitioner Reports to Police That He Was 'Detained and Beaten'" [Fangmin baojing cheng zao "guanya ouda"], Beijing News, 12 January 11; "Black Jails, Petitioners on Eve of Spring Festival: 13 Big Stories of Beijing Petitioning in 2010" [Hei jianyu, fang min chunwan: 2010 nian zaijing fang min 13 da xinwen], Boxun, 3 January 11; Liu Chang, "Controversy Over 'Black Jails' Continues," Global Times, 4 May 11;

"After All, Where Is Jiangsu Sihong County's 'Petitioner Study Class'?" [Jiangsu si hong xian de "xinfang xuexi ban" jiujing shige shenme difang?], Southern Metropolitan Daily, 28 April 11; Andrew Jacobs and Jonathan Ansfield, "Well-Oiled Security Apparatus in China Stifles Calls for Change," New York Times, 28 February 11; Melinda Liu and Isaac Stone Fish, "Portrait of the Gulag," Newsweek, 26 June 11; "Veterans Protest Over Welfare," Radio Free Asia, 29 June 11.

[126] Long Zhi, "Anyuanding: Investigation Into Beijing's 'Black Jails' To Stop Petitioners" [Anyuanding: beijing jie fang "hei jianyu" diaocha], Southern Metropolitan Daily, 24 September 10; "China Police Investigate 'Black Jails' for Protesters," BBC, 27 September 10.

[127] Andrew Jacobs, "China Investigates Extralegal Petitioner Detentions," New York Times, 27 September 10; Susan Stumme, "China PM First To Meet Petitioners in 60 Years," Agence France-Presse, reprinted in Google, 25 January 11.

[128] Zhan Caiqiang, "'Study Sessions' Nightmare" ["Xuexi ban" mengyan], Southern Metropolitan Daily, 27 April 11. See also Liu Chang, "Controversy Over 'Black Jails' Continues," Global Times, 4 May 11.

[129] The term "nail household" (dingzi hu) is commonly used to refer to tenants who refuse to leave their households despite the demolition of structures around them.

[130] Zhan Caiqiang, "'Study Sessions' Nightmare" ["Xuexi ban" mengyan], Southern Metropolitan Daily, 27 April 11. See also Liu Chang, "Controversy Over 'Black Jails' Continues," Global Times, 4 May 11.

[131] Zhan Caiqiang, "'Study Sessions' Nightmare" ["Xuexi ban" mengyan], Southern Metropolitan Daily, 27 April 11; Zhang Xuanchen, "Officials Accused of Opening Illegal 'Jail,'" Shanghai Daily, 28 April 11.

[132] An Ying and Yi Fangxing, "Woman Detained in Black Jail After Coming to Beijing To Handle Affairs" [Laijing banshi nu bei guan heijianyu], Beijing News, 2 August 11; Wang Huazhong, "Former Inmate Reveals Existence of 'Black Jail,'" China Daily, 3 August 11.

[133] Ibid.

[134] Ibid.

[135] Dui Hua Foundation, "Official Fear: Inside a Shuanggui Investigation Facility," 5 July 11.

[136] Li Yanhui, "Chaoyang Deputy Director Allegedly Detained for Bribery," Global Times, 2 June 11; Zhang Lu, "Beijing's Chaoyang District Deputy Mayor Liu Xiquan Investigated," Caijing, 1 June 11.

[137] "Shandong Provincial Government Secretary-General Zhang Wanqing Dismissed, Had Been Detained Under Shuanggui" [Shandong sheng zhengfu mishu zhang zhang wanqing bei ti qing chezhi ci qian bei shuanggui], People's Daily, 26 May 11.

[138] Zhang Yuzhe, "High-Ranking Ministry of Finance Official Detained," Caixin Net, 18 January 11.

[139] "Human Rights and the Rule of Law in China," CECC Hearing, 20 September 06, Testimony of Jerome A. Cohen, Professor of Law, New York University Law School, Co-Director of U.S.-Asia Law Institute.

[140] Dui Hua Foundation, "Official Fear: Inside a Shuanggui Investigation Facility," 5 July 11.

[141] "Human Rights and the Rule of Law in China," CECC Hearing, 20 September 06, Testimony of Jerome A. Cohen, Professor of Law, New York University Law School, Co-Director of U.S.-Asia Law Institute.

[142] CECC, 2010 Annual Report, 10 October 10, 96.

[143] He Weifang, "For the Rule of Law, for the Ideal in Our Hearts—A Letter to Chongqing Colleagues" [Weile fazhi, weile women xinzhongde di na yi fen lixiang—zhi chongqing falu jie de yifeng gongkaixin], China Media Project, 12 April 11.

[144] Ibid.

[145] Ibid.

[146] Bureau of Democracy, Human Rights, and Labor, U.S. Department of State, "Country Report on Human Rights Practices—2010 Human Rights Report: China (includes Tibet, Hong Kong, and Macau)," 8 April 11.

[147] "Jailed Activist's Health Failing," Radio Free Asia, 17 January 11.

[148] Ibid.; Chinese Human Rights Defenders, "Zeng Jinyan Once Again Applies for Medical Parole for Hu Jia's Condition in Prison," 17 January 11.

[149] PEN International, "CHINA: Death Announced of Prominent Writer Zhang Jianhong (aka Li Hong)," 12 January 11.

[150] Ibid.

[151] "China Frees Father Zhao Lianhai Jailed for Milk Protest," Associated Press, reprinted in Australian, 29 December 10.

[152] Ibid.

[153] Will Clem and Choi Chi-yuk, "Beijing's Silence an Ominous Signal," South China Morning Post, 6 April 11; "Milk Activist Told 'Be Quiet or Go Back to Jail,'" South China Morning Post, 8 April 11.

[154] "Milk Activist Told 'Be Quiet or Go Back to Jail,'" South China Morning Post, 8 April 11.

[155] Human Rights in China, "Petitioner Recounts Abuses During RTL; Medical Parole Rescinded," 24 February 11.

[156] Ibid.

[157] "Mao Hengfeng: Amnesty Urgent Action," Guardian, 25 June 11.

[158] "Supreme People's Court Work Report" [Zuigao renmin fayuan gongzuo baogao], Xinhua, reprinted in National People's Congress of the People's Republic of China, 19 March 11.

[159] Supreme People's Court, "2010 Annual Work Report on the People's Courts" [Renminfayuan gongzuo niandu baogao (2010 nian)], 25 May 11. For more information on the death penalty in the 2010 Annual Work Report, see, e.g., Michael Bristow, "China Orders Suspension of Death Sentences," BBC News, 25 May 11; Wang Qiushi, "SPC Requests Uniform Suitable Standards for the Death Penalty; Try Utmost To Not Immediately Implement the

23

Death Penalty" [Zuigao fa yaoqiu tongyi sixing shiyong biaozhun jinliang bu pan sixing liji zhixing], People's Daily, 25 May 11.

[160] Zhao Yinan, "13 Crimes Removed From Death Penalty List," China Daily, 26 February 11; Robert Saiget, "China Scraps Death Penalty for Some Crimes," Agence France-Presse, reprinted in Google, 26 February 11.

[161] Zhao Yinan, "13 Crimes Removed From Death Penalty List," China Daily, 26 February 11; "China Mulls Lessening Number of Crimes Punishable by Death," Xinhua, 23 August 10.

[162] Zhao Lei, "Greater Steps Can Be Taken To Reduce the Death Penalty" [Jianshao sizui, buzi keyi zai da yixie], Southern Weekend, 26 August 10. For more information, see "Chinese Government Considers Reducing Number of Crimes Punishable by Death," Congressional-Executive Commission on China, 23 February 11.

○